FUSS-FREE
FILIPINO
FOOD

QUICK & EASY DISHES
FOR EVERYDAY COOKING

ANGELO COMSTI

 **Marshall Cavendish**
Cuisine

Food preparation, styling and photography by Angelo Comsti
Author's portrait by Anthony Prudencio

Published by Marshall Cavendish Cuisine
An imprint of Marshall Cavendish International

Other Marshall Cavendish Offices:
99 White Plains Road, Tarrytown NY 10591-9001, USA • Marshall Cavendish
International (Thailand) Co Ltd. 253 Asoke, 12th Flr, Sukhumvit 21 Road, Klongtoey
Nua, Wattana, Bangkok 10110, Thailand • Marshall Cavendish (Malaysia) Sdn Bhd,
Times Subang, Lot 46, Subang Hi-Tech Industrial Park, Batu Tiga, 40000 Shah
Alam, Selangor Darul Ehsan, Malaysia

Marshall Cavendish is a trademark of Times Publishing Limited

National Library Board, Singapore Cataloguing-in-Publication Data

Comsti, Angelo F., author.
Fuss-free Filipino food : quick & easy dishes for everyday cooking / Angelo Comsti.
– Singapore : Marshall Cavendish Cuisine, [2015]
pages cm
ISBN : 978-981-4721-50-9 (paperback)

1. Cooking, Philippine. 2. Cookbooks. I. Title.

TX724.5.P5
641.59599 -- dc23   OCN922018094

Printed by Times Offset (M) Sdn Bhd

This book is for the ones feeding my zest for life:
my family, the inspiring local food
community and my country.

CONTENTS

INTRODUCTION

Quick. Easy. Simple.

For a busy working parent with mouths to feed, these words are music to the ears. For a newlywed who aims for domestic bliss or someone who is just learning how to cook, these words offer countless possibilities. For a Filipino working abroad or someone who is keen on sampling Filipino cuisine, these words promise good memories.

Whereas my books before were composed of dishes born out of old, personal stories, *Fuss-free Filipino Food* will provide inspiration for making new ones.

I hope that this book will drive you to don that apron, get busy in the kitchen and enjoy home-grown flavours in the quickest, easiest and simplest way.

Happy cooking!

Angelo

VEGETABLES

ENSALADANG PAKO FIDDLEHEAD FERN SALAD

SERVES 4

500 g fiddlehead fern
1¹/₂ Tbsp vinegar
¹/₄ cup olive oil
Salt and pepper, to taste
1 small yellow onion, peeled and sliced
3 tomatoes, chopped
A handful of pork crackling (*chicharon*), crushed

Wash fiddlehead fern well, then cut off and discard tough bottom stems, leaving 5–7-cm of stems from the tip.

Boil a pot of water and blanch fern lightly. Drain and set aside.

In a bowl, combine vinegar and olive oil. Whisk to combine. Adjust to taste with salt and pepper.

In a mixing bowl, combine fern, onion and tomatoes. Add vinaigrette and toss to mix. Transfer to a serving plate.

Top with pork crackling. Serve.

MONGGO MUNG BEAN SOUP

SERVES 4

1 cup mung beans, rinsed and drained
3¹/₂ cups water
2 Tbsp cooking oil
100 g pork, cut into short, thin strips
3 cloves garlic, peeled and minced
1 small yellow onion, peeled and minced
3 medium tomatoes, chopped
2 Tbsp dried shrimp (*hibi*), crushed
60 g moringga leaves
Fish sauce, to taste

Place mung beans and water in a pot and bring to a boil over medium heat. Let boil until mung beans are tender.

Meanwhile, heat oil in a pan over medium heat. Add pork and sauté until cooked.

Add garlic, onion, tomatoes and dried shrimp. Sauté for a minute.

Add mixture to pot and return to the boil.

Add moringga leaves and simmer for a minute. Adjust to taste with fish sauce.

Dish up and serve.

GINATAANG KALABASA AT SITAW
SQUASH AND LONG BEANS IN COCONUT CREAM

SERVES 4

2 Tbsp cooking oil

2 cloves garlic, peeled and minced

1 small yellow onion, peeled and chopped

1 cup coconut milk

2 tsp fish sauce + more if necessary

500 g squash, cut into cubes

150 g long beans (*sitaw*), cut into 5-cm lengths

$1/2$ cup coconut cream

Heat oil in a pot over medium heat. Add garlic and onion and sauté until onion is soft and translucent.

Add coconut milk and fish sauce. Stir.

Add squash and lower heat. Simmer until squash is close to being tender.

Add long beans. When long beans are tender, add coconut cream. Adjust to taste with fish sauce.

Dish up and serve.

GISING-GISING GREEN BEANS IN COCONUT CREAM

SERVES 4

2 Tbsp cooking oil
2 cloves garlic, peeled and minced
1 small yellow onion, peeled and chopped
300 g minced pork
2 Tbsp shrimp paste
1 cup coconut cream
300 g green beans, chopped
1 red bird's eye chilli, chopped
Salt and pepper, to taste

Heat oil in a pan over medium heat. Add garlic and onion and sauté until onion is soft and translucent.

Add minced pork and cook until it starts to render oil.

Add shrimp paste and mix well.

Add coconut cream and mix again.

Add green beans and chilli. Cook until beans are tender. Season with salt and pepper.

Dish up and serve.

PINAKBET VEGETABLE STEW

SERVES 4

2 Tbsp cooking oil

50 g pork belly, cut into strips

3 cloves garlic, peeled and minced

1 small yellow onion, peeled and sliced

2 medium tomatoes, chopped

2 Tbsp shrimp paste

1¼ cups water

150 g squash, cut into cubes

100 g baby bitter gourd (*ampalaya*),
   white membrane removed and sliced

3 baby okra (ladies' fingers), sliced

1 small eggplant (aubergine), sliced

2 stalks long beans (*sitaw*), cut to 5-cm lengths

Salt and pepper, to taste

Heat oil in a pan over medium heat. Add pork belly and sauté until golden brown and cooked. Set aside.

In the same pan, sauté garlic and onion until onion is soft and translucent.

Add tomatoes and sauté until tomatoes are soft. Add shrimp paste and mix well.

Add water and bring to a boil. Add vegetables and cook until tender.

Return fried pork belly to pot. Season with salt and pepper.

Dish up and serve.

RICE AND NOODLES

ARROZ CALDO CHICKEN AND RICE PORRIDGE
SERVES 4

1¹/₂ cups glutinous rice
2 Tbsp cooking oil
3 cloves garlic, peeled and minced
5-cm knob ginger, peeled and minced
1 small yellow onion, peeled and chopped
6 cups water
¹/₂ Tbsp fish sauce
500 g chicken parts
1 spring onion, chopped
Crisp-fried garlic, to garnish

Wash glutinous rice and let soak in a bowl with water.

Heat oil in a pot over medium heat. Add garlic, ginger and onion and sauté until onion is soft and translucent.

Add water and fish sauce and bring to a boil.

Add chicken and cook for about 12 minutes or until chicken is cooked. Remove chicken from pot and set aside to cool before shredding meat. Discard bones.

Remove half the chicken stock and freeze for use in other recipes.

Drain glutinous rice and add to pot. Bring to a boil, then lower heat and simmer until rice is tender.

Remove pot from heat. Add chicken meat to pot and mix well. Taste and add more fish sauce if necessary.

Garnish with spring onion and fried garlic. Serve with a condiment of fish sauce and calamansi juice.

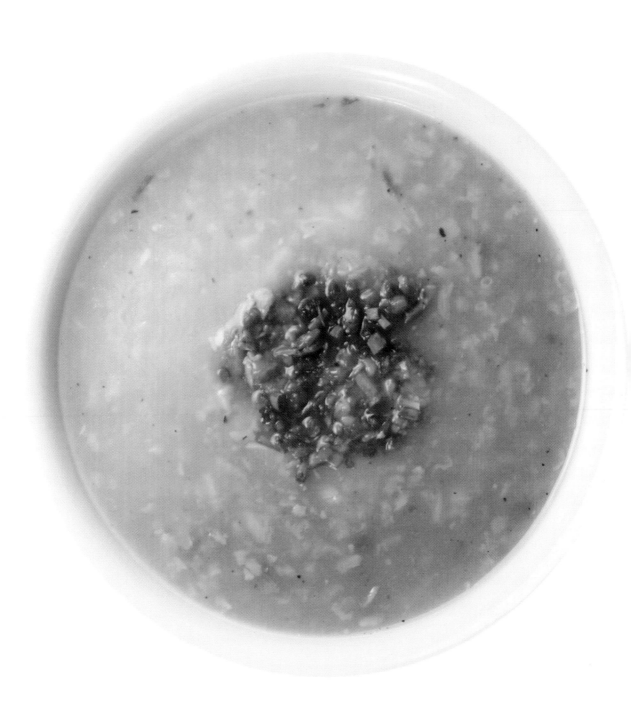

PANCIT BIHON STIR-FRIED FINE RICE NOODLES

SERVES 4

240 g fine rice noodles (*pancit bihon*)
2 Tbsp cooking oil
3 cloves garlic, peeled and minced
1 small yellow onion, peeled and sliced
2 cups chicken stock
1/4 head cabbage, finely sliced
1 medium carrot, peeled and cut to strips
4 Tbsp light soy sauce
1 chicken breast, cooked and shredded
Salt and pepper, to taste
5 calamansi limes, halved

Soak rice noodles in a basin of warm water for about 7 minutes or until softened. Drain and set aside.

Heat oil in a deep pan over medium heat. Add garlic and onion and sauté until onion is soft and translucent.

Add chicken stock and let simmer.

Add cabbage and carrot. Cook until tender.

Add rice noodles and soy sauce. Toss to mix.

Add shredded chicken. Season with salt and pepper.

Serve with sliced calamansi halves.

PANCIT LUGLOG THICK RICE NOODLES WITH ANNATTO SAUCE

SERVES 4

500 g thick rice noodles

$1/4$ cup annatto oil (page 40)

3 cloves garlic, peeled and minced

$1/4$ cup plain (all-purpose) flour

3 cups fish stock

2 Tbsp fish sauce

250 g prawns, peeled, deveined and cooked

$1/2$ cup smoked fish, flaked

A handful of pork crackling (*chicharon*), crushed

1 spring onion, chopped

Prepare rice noodles according to packet instructions. Drain and set aside on a serving plate.

Heat annatto oil in a deep pan over medium heat. Add garlic and cook until golden brown.

Add flour and mix until combined, then continue to cook for a minute.

Add fish stock and fish sauce and whisk until combined and mixture is thick.

Ladle annatto sauce over noodles.

Top with cooked prawns, smoked fish, pork crackling and spring onion.

Serve.

PANCIT LOMI EGG NOODLES IN SOUP

SERVES 4

2 Tbsp cooking oil

2 cloves garlic, peeled and minced

1 small yellow onion, peeled and chopped

250 g minced pork

3 cups chicken stock

500 g fresh egg noodles, cooked

1 small carrot, peeled and cut into strips

$^1/_2$ head small cabbage, finely sliced

Salt and pepper, to taste

2 eggs, beaten

Heat oil in a pan over medium heat. Add garlic and onion and sauté until onion is soft and translucent.

Add minced pork and sauté until brown. Add chicken stock and bring to a boil.

Add egg noodles, carrot and cabbage. Season with salt and pepper.

When vegetables are tender, add eggs. Remove from heat.

Mix and serve.

POULTRY

PININYAHANG MANOK PINEAPPLE CHICKEN

SERVES 4

500 g chicken breast fillet, cut into strips
Salt and pepper, to taste
2 Tbsp cooking oil
4 cloves garlic, peeled and minced
1 small yellow onion, peeled and chopped
1 Tbsp fish sauce
1 can (420 g) pineapple chunks, drained
³/₄ cup water
3 Tbsp sweetened condensed milk
1 spring onion, chopped

Season chicken with salt and pepper.

Heat oil in a deep pan over medium heat. Add garlic and onion and sauté until onion is soft and translucent.

Add chicken and cook until chicken is lightly coloured.

Add fish sauce and pineapple chunks. Sauté for a minute.

Add water and condensed milk and mix well. Lower heat and simmer for a minute. Adjust to taste with salt and pepper.

Dish up and garnish with spring onion. Serve.

TINOLANG MANOK
CHICKEN IN GINGER SOUP

SERVES 4

2 Tbsp cooking oil

2 cloves garlic, peeled and minced

5-cm knob ginger, peeled and cut into strips

1 medium yellow onion, peeled and chopped

800 g chicken parts

4 cups water

2 Tbsp fish sauce

400 g unripe green papaya, peeled,
    seeded and cut into cubes

A handful of chilli leaves

Salt and pepper to taste

Heat oil in a deep pan over medium heat. Add garlic, ginger and onion and sauté until onion is soft and translucent.

Add chicken and cook until chicken is lightly coloured.

Add water and fish sauce and bring to a boil, then lower heat and simmer until chicken is cooked through.

Add green papaya and continue simmering until papaya is tender.

Add chilli leaves. Adjust to taste with salt and pepper.

Dish up and serve.

BINAKOL NA MANOK CHICKEN IN COCONUT WATER

SERVES 4

750 g chicken breast
Salt and pepper, to taste
2 Tbsp cooking oil
2 cloves garlic, peeled and minced
5-cm knob ginger, peeled and minced
1 small yellow onion, peeled and sliced
1 stalk lemongrass (white part only), pounded
1^1/$_2$–2 cups fresh coconut juice
Fish sauce, to taste
A handful of chilli leaves
3 young coconuts, flesh extracted and cut into large pieces

Season chicken with salt and pepper.

Heat oil in a deep pan over medium heat. Add garlic, ginger and onion and sauté until onion is soft and translucent.

Add chicken and cook until lightly coloured.

Add lemongrass and coconut juice. Lower heat and simmer until chicken is cooked through.

Adjust to taste with fish sauce.

Add chilli leaves and coconut flesh. Leave for a minute to heat through.

Dish up and serve.

POCHERONG MANOK CHICKEN IN TOMATO SAUCE

SERVES 4

2 Tbsp cooking oil

2 cloves garlic, peeled and minced

1 small yellow onion, peeled and thinly sliced

750 g chicken parts

1 Tbsp fish sauce

1 cup tomato sauce

2^1/$_2$ cups water

Salt and pepper, to taste

2 medium potatoes, peeled and cut into cubes

4 cardava bananas (saba), peeled and sliced

1 small cabbage, chopped

1 bunch bok choy (pechay), ends trimmed and leaves separated

Heat oil in a deep pan over medium heat. Add garlic and onion and sauté until onion is soft and translucent.

Add chicken and season with fish sauce. Cook until chicken is lightly browned and juices run clear.

Add tomato sauce and water. Bring to a boil, then lower heat and simmer until chicken is cooked through. Adjust to taste with salt and pepper.

Add potatoes and bananas. When potatoes are close to being tender, add cabbage and bok choy.

Dish up and serve.

INASAL NA MANOK BACOLOD-STYLE GRILLED CHICKEN

SERVES 4

4 cloves garlic, peeled and chopped

8 calamansi limes, juice extracted

1 tsp crushed black peppercorns

2 stalks lemongrass (white part only), chopped

$1/2$ cup vinegar

1 Tbsp sugar

4 whole chicken legs

1 cup vegetable oil

$1/2$ cup annatto seeds

Bamboo skewers, as needed

In a bowl, combine garlic, calamansi juice, peppercorns, lemongrass, vinegar and sugar. Stir to combine.

Add chicken legs, cover and refrigerate for 20 minutes.

Prepare annatto oil. Place vegetable oil and annatto seeds in a small pot and heat until it comes to a shallow simmer. Remove from heat and set aside to infuse for 10 minutes. Strain.

Skewer marinated chicken legs with barbecue skewers.

Heat a barbecue and grill chicken legs until cooked through, turning and basting with annatto oil frequently.

Serve.

FISH AND SEAFOOD

KINILAW NA TUNA CURED TUNA

SERVES 4

750 g sashimi-grade tuna fillet, cut into cubes

1 small red onion, peeled and finely diced

1 medium red bell pepper (capsicum),
   cored, seeded and finely diced

1 medium green bell pepper (capsicum),
   cored, seeded and finely diced

2.5-cm knob ginger, peeled and minced

$^1/_2$ cup vinegar

1 Tbsp sugar

1 red bird's eye chilli, finely chopped

A pinch of salt

In a bowl, combine tuna, onion, bell peppers and ginger. Toss.

In another bowl, stir together vinegar, sugar and chilli until sugar
is dissolved.

Pour vinegar mixture over tuna. Toss and season with a pinch
of salt.

Serve.

UKOY NA DULONG SILVER FISH FRITTERS

SERVES 4

1 medium egg, beaten
1 cup plain (all-purpose) flour
1¼ cups water
A pinch of salt
500 g fresh silver fish (*dulong*)
Cooking oil, as needed

In a bowl, combine egg, flour, water and salt. Stir until batter is smooth.

Add silver fish and gently mix until well combined.

Heat a little oil in a pan over medium heat.

Drop ¼ cup batter into pan and spread to make a thin pancake. Cook until golden brown on one side before flipping over to brown the other side. Transfer to a plate lined with paper towels.

Repeat until batter is used up.

Serve.

SUAM NA MAIS AT HALAAN
CORN AND CLAM SOUP

SERVES 4

1 cup + $^1/_2$ cup whole corn kernels
2 Tbsp cooking oil
2 cloves garlic, peeled and minced
2.5-cm knob ginger, peeled and minced
1 small yellow onion, peeled and minced
4 cups chicken stock
500 g clams (*halaan*)
A handful of chilli leaves
Fish sauce, to taste

Place 1 cup corn kernels into a blender and purée. Set aside.

Heat oil in a pot and sauté garlic, ginger and onion until onion is soft and translucent.

Add chicken stock, corn purée and remaining corn kernels. Stir.

Add clams, cover pot and let cook until clams have opened. Discard any that do not open.

Add chilli leaves and fish sauce to taste.

Dish up and serve.

FISH ESCABECHE SWEET AND SOUR FISH

SERVES 4

1 kg grouper (*lapu-lapu*), cleaned
Salt, as needed
5 Tbsp cooking oil, divided
2 cloves garlic, peeled and minced
2.5-cm knob ginger, peeled and chopped
1 small red onion, peeled and chopped
1 cup vinegar
3 Tbsp brown sugar
1 Tbsp cornflour, mixed with 3 Tbsp water
A dash of ground white pepper
1 red bell pepper (capsicum), cored, seeded and sliced
1 green bell pepper (capsicum), cored, seeded and sliced
1 small carrot, peeled and sliced

Season fish with salt. Set aside.

Heat 4 Tbsp oil in a pan over medium heat.

Lower fish gently into pan and cook until golden brown on
one side before turning fish over to cook the other side until
the tip of a knife goes through the thickest part of the fish easily.
Transfer to a serving plate.

Reheat pan with 1 Tbsp oil. Add garlic, ginger and onion and sauté
until onion is soft and translucent.

Add vinegar, brown sugar and cornflour slurry. Season with
salt and pepper. Stir until liquid thickens.

Add bell peppers and carrot. Mix well and pour over fried fish.

Serve.

PAKSIW NA BANGUS BELLY MILKFISH BELLY IN VINEGAR

SERVES 4

4 cloves garlic, peeled and crushed

2.5-cm knob ginger, peeled, sliced and pounded

1 small yellow onion, peeled and thinly sliced

$^1/_2$ cup vinegar

1 cup water

2 green chillies

4 whole black peppercorns

4 milkfish belly fillets

100 g baby bitter gourd (*ampalaya*),
   white membrane removed and sliced

Place garlic, ginger, onion, vinegar, water, chillies and peppercorns
in a pot and bring to a boil over medium heat.

Lower heat and add milkfish fillets. Cover and let simmer
until fish is cooked.

Add bitter gourd. Simmer for another 2 minutes or until bitter gourd
is tender.

Dish up and serve.

SINIGANG NA HIPON PRAWNS IN SOUR SOUP

SERVES 4

3 cups water + more if desired

500 g unripe tamarind

2 tomatoes, cut into quarters

1 medium yellow onion, peeled and cut into quarters

300 g prawns

3 long beans (*sitaw*), cut to 5-cm lengths

A handful of water spinach (*kangkong*)

2 Tbsp fish sauce

Place 3 cups water and tamarind in a pot and bring to a boil over medium heat. Lower heat and let simmer for 30 minutes.

Remove tamarind and press through a strainer to extract juice. Add extracted juice to pot and bring tamarind stock back to a simmer. Add water if desired.

Add tomatoes, onion and prawns and cook for about 5 minutes or until prawns change colour and are cooked.

Add long beans and water spinach and cook for another minute. Season with fish sauce.

Dish up and serve.

MEAT

PORK BARBECUE

SERVES 4

500 g pork belly
¹/₂ cup light soy sauce
¹/₂ cup pineapple juice
3 calamansi limes, juice extracted
1 tsp freshly cracked black pepper
2 red bird's eye chillies, chopped
Bamboo skewers, as needed

Freeze pork belly. Cut into long, thin strips. Set aside to thaw.

In a bowl, combine soy sauce, pineapple juice, calamansi juice, pepper and chillies. Mix well.

Place pork belly strips into marinade. Mix well, cover and set aside for 20 minutes.

Thread pork belly strips through bamboo skewers. Reserve marinade.

Heat a barbecue and grill pork belly for about 10 minutes or until cooked through, turning and basting with reserved marinade frequently.

Serve.

LECHON KAWALI DEEP-FRIED PORK BELLY

SERVES 4

750 g pork belly
Water, as needed
1 bay leaf
3 whole black peppercorns
1 small onion, peeled and quartered
Cooking oil for deep-frying

Slice pork belly into cubes and place into a pot. Add sufficient water to submerge pork belly.

Add bay leaf, peppercorns and onion. Cover and bring to a boil, then lower heat and simmer for about 20 minutes or until tender.

Drain and transfer pork belly to a plate. Set aside to cool. Pat dry.

Heat oil for deep-frying over low heat. Gently lower pork into hot oil and deep-fry until golden brown. Remove and set aside to drain on paper towels for 10 minutes.

Reheat oil and deep-fry a second time over medium-high heat until skin is crisp.

Remove and drain well on paper towels.

Slice and serve.

PORK ADOBO
PORK IN
SOY SAUCE
AND VINEGAR
SERVES 4

750 g pork shoulder, cut into cubes
$^3/_4$ cup light soy sauce
$^3/_4$ cup vinegar
3 cloves garlic, peeled and crushed
2 bay leaves
6 whole black peppercorns
Salt and pepper to taste

Place pork cubes into a pot with soy sauce, vinegar, garlic, bay leaves and peppercorns.

Bring to a boil over high heat, then lower heat and simmer for 30 minutes or until tender, skimming away any scum that rises.

Adjust to taste with salt and pepper.

Dish up and serve.

BICOL EXPRESS PORK IN COCONUT MILK

SERVES 4

2 Tbsp cooking oil

2.5-cm ginger, peeled and minced

3 cloves garlic, peeled and minced

1 small yellow onion, peeled and minced

400 g pork shoulder, cut into cubes

1¹/₂ Tbsp shrimp paste

400 ml coconut milk

2 green chillies, sliced

1 red bird's eye chilli, chopped

Salt and pepper to taste

Heat oil in a pan over medium heat. Add ginger, garlic and onion and sauté until onion is soft and translucent.

Add pork and sauté until brown on all sides.

Add shrimp paste and mix well. Add coconut milk and bring to a boil.

Add chillies and adjust to taste with salt and pepper.

Dish up and serve.

LECHON PAKSIW ROAST PORK IN LIVER SAUCE

SERVES 4

2 Tbsp cooking oil
5 cloves garlic, peeled and minced
1 medium yellow onion, peeled and chopped
500 g roast pork, cut into cubes
1¹/₂ cups water
1 bay leaf
7 whole black peppercorns
2 Tbsp vinegar
1 cup liver sauce

Heat oil in a pan over medium heat. Add garlic and onion and sauté until onion is soft and translucent.

Add roast pork and sauté for a minute.

Add water, bay leaf and peppercorns. Bring to a boil, then lower heat and simmer until liquid is reduced by half.

Add vinegar and mix well. Add liver sauce and mix again. Return to a simmer before dishing up.

Serve.

PORK MENUDO PORK AND CHICKPEAS IN TOMATO SAUCE

SERVES 4

2 Tbsp cooking oil

2 cloves garlic, peeled and chopped

1 small yellow onion, peeled and chopped

500 g pork shoulder, cut into cubes

400 g tomatoes, chopped

1 cup tomato sauce

1 medium potato, peeled and cut into cubes

1 cup canned chickpeas, drained

1 red bell pepper (capsicum), cored and cut into
    squares the size of potato cubes

1 green bell pepper (capsicum), cored and cut into
    squares the size of potato cubes

Salt and pepper to taste

Heat oil in a pot over medium heat. Add garlic and onion and sauté until onion is soft and translucent.

Add pork cubes and sauté until brown on all sides.

Add tomatoes, lower heat and simmer for 5 minutes.

Add tomato sauce and mix. Let simmer until pork is cooked through.

Add potato cubes and cook until tender.

Add chickpeas and bell peppers. Cook for a minute.

Adjust to taste with salt and pepper.

Dish up and serve.

BINAGOONGANG BABOY PORK IN SHRIMP PASTE

SERVES 4

500 g pork shoulder, cut into cubes
¹/₃ cup vinegar
1 cup water
1 bay leaf
2 Tbsp cooking oil
3 cloves garlic, peeled and minced
1 small yellow onion, peeled and chopped
2 medium tomatoes, chopped
2–3 Tbsp shrimp paste
1 green chilli, sliced

Place pork cubes in a pot with vinegar, water and bay leaf. Bring to a boil over medium heat, then lower heat and simmer until meat is tender, skimming away any scum that rises.

Drain pork and set aside.

Heat oil in a pan over medium heat. Add garlic and onion and sauté until onion is soft and translucent.

Add tomatoes and cook until wilted.

Add shrimp paste, cooked pork and green chilli. Mix well.

Dish up and serve.

DINUGUAN PORK BLOOD STEW

SERVES 4

2 Tbsp cooking oil

2 cloves garlic, peeled and minced

2.5-cm knob ginger, peeled and minced

1 small yellow onion, peeled and chopped

500 g shoulder pork, cut into cubes

1 Tbsp fish sauce

1^1/$_2$ cups water

1^1/$_2$ cups pig's blood

3 Tbsp vinegar

2 green chillies, sliced

1 tsp sugar

Salt and pepper to taste

Heat oil in a deep pan over medium heat. Add garlic, ginger and onion and sauté until onion is soft and translucent.

Add pork and sauté until brown on all sides. Season with fish sauce.

Add water and bring to a boil, then lower heat and simmer until pork is cooked through, skimming away any scum that rises.

In a bowl, combine pig's blood and vinegar. Stir well. Add to pan and bring to a boil, stirring continuously until sauce is slightly thick.

Adjust to taste with salt and pepper.

Dish up and serve.

ADOBONG PUTI PORK IN VINEGAR

SERVES 4

2 Tbsp cooking oil
500 g pork belly, sliced
3 cloves garlic, peeled and crushed
$^{1}/_{2}$ cup vinegar
$1^{1}/_{2}$ cups water
5 whole black peppercorns
1 bay leaf

Heat oil in a pan over medium heat. Add pork belly and cook until brown on both sides.

Add garlic and sauté until just beginning to brown.

Add vinegar, water, peppercorns and bay leaf. Lower heat and simmer until pork is cooked through.

Dish up and serve.

PICADILLO PORK AND WINGED BEAN SOUP

SERVES 4

2 Tbsp cooking oil
1 small yellow onion, peeled and minced
3 cloves garlic, peeled and minced
1 large ripe tomato, diced
500 g minced pork
Salt and pepper to taste
150 g winged beans (*sigarilyas*), sliced
2¹/₂ cups water
Fish sauce, to taste

Heat oil in a pot over medium heat. Add onion, garlic and tomato and sauté until onion is soft and translucent.

Add minced pork and sauté, breaking up any lumps. Season with salt and pepper.

Add winged beans and sauté for another minute.

Add water and let boil until winged beans are tender. Adjust to taste with fish sauce.

Dish up and serve.

LUMPIANG SHANGHAI FRIED PORK SPRING ROLLS

MAKES ABOUT 50

150 g minced pork
1/2 cup minced carrot
1/4 cup minced yellow onion
1/2 Tbsp garlic powder
2 eggs, beaten
A dash of ground white pepper
A pinch of salt
50 sheets spring roll wrapper (small)
Cooking oil for deep-frying
Sweet and sour sauce, to taste

In a bowl, combine minced pork, carrot, onion, garlic powder and eggs. Mix well. Season with salt and pepper.

Spoon 2 tsp mixture across one corner of a spring roll wrapper. Fold corner over mixture, then fold in left and right corners to enclose mixture. Roll up firmly and seal with water.

Repeat until ingredients are used up.

Heat oil for deep-frying over medium heat. Lower spring rolls gently into hot oil and cook until golden brown and crisp. Remove and drain well on paper towels.

Serve with sweet and sour sauce.

BISTEK TAGALOG
BEEF STEAK WITH ONIONS

SERVES 4

500 g beef sirloin
$^1/_2$ cup light soy sauce
5 calamansi limes, juice extracted
$^1/_2$ tsp freshly cracked black pepper
2 Tbsp cooking oil
1 large yellow onion, peeled and cut into rings

Cut beef thinly. Set aside.

In a bowl, combine soy sauce, calamansi juice and black pepper. Add beef and mix well. Cover and refrigerate for at least 30 minutes.

Heat oil in a pan over low-medium heat. Add onion and sauté until onion is slightly wilted. Transfer to a plate.

Drain beef and reserve marinade.

Reheat pan and sauté beef until colour changes and meat is lightly cooked. Add marinade and cook until slightly reduced.

Top with cooked onion.

Dish up and serve.

TAPA CURED BEEF

SERVES 4

2 cloves garlic, peeled and chopped
1 Tbsp sugar
$1/2$ cup light soy sauce
$1/2$ tsp ground black pepper
350 g thinly sliced beef for sukiyaki
2 Tbsp cooking oil

In a bowl, combine garlic, sugar, soy sauce and pepper.
Stir to dissolve sugar.

Place in a sealable container along with beef. Refrigerate overnight.

Drain beef.

Heat oil in a pan over medium heat. Add beef and cook for about
a minute on each side.

Dish up and serve.

SNACKS AND DESSERTS

YEMA SWEET CUSTARD CANDY

MAKES ABOUT 30 PIECES

5 egg yolks, beaten
168 ml sweetened condensed milk
$1/2$ tsp grated lime zest
1 tsp butter
Sugar, as needed

Combine all ingredients in a small pan over low to medium heat. Stir continuously until mixture is thick and dense, and starts to pull away from the sides of the pan.

Transfer to a plate and let cool.

When mixture is cool, take a teaspoonful of the mixture and form into a ball. Repeat until mixture is used up.

Coat balls with sugar and set aside to harden.

Serve.

FILIPINO FRUIT SALAD

SERVES 4

3 cups canned fruit cocktail, drained
1/2 cup nata de coco
3 Tbsp sweetened condensed milk
1 cup heavy cream

In a salad bowl, combine fruit cocktail and nata de coco and mix well.

In a small bowl, stir together condensed milk and cream. Add to fruit mixture and mix well.

Cover and refrigerate for 20 minutes.

Serve chilled.

MINATAMIS NA SAGING AT SABA
BANANA AND SAGO PEARLS IN SYRUP

SERVES 4

1 cup sago pearls
$^1/_2$ cup water
$^3/_4$ cup brown sugar
1 pandan leaf, cleaned and knotted
6 cardava bananas (*saba*), peeled and sliced

Boil a pot of water over medium heat and add sago pearls. Cover and let boil for an hour, stirring every 10 minutes until sago is translucent. Top up with more water as necessary. Drain and set aside.

Combine $^1/_2$ cup water, brown sugar and pandan leaf in a small pot over low to medium heat. Cook, stirring until sugar is dissolved.

Add bananas and cook for about 12 minutes or until bananas are soft. Remove from heat.

Add sago and mix. Set aside to cool.

Serve.

TURON
FRIED BANANA
SPRING ROLLS

SERVES 4

6 cardava bananas (*saba*),
  peeled and halved lengthwise

3 Tbsp brown sugar

12 sheets spring roll wrapper

Cooking oil for deep-frying

Coat bananas with brown sugar.

Place a slice of banana across one corner of a spring roll wrapper. Fold corner over banana, then fold in left and right corners to enclose banana. Roll up firmly and seal with water.

Repeat until ingredients are used up.

Heat oil for deep-frying over medium heat. Lower spring rolls gently into hot oil and cook until golden brown and crisp. Remove and drain well on paper towels.

Serve.

MARUYA BANANA FRITTERS

SERVES 4

$^1/_2$ **cup plain (all-purpose) flour**

$^1/_2$ **tsp baking soda**

1 egg, beaten

$^1/_2$ **cup water**

**4 cardava bananas (*saba*),
    peeled and halved lengthwise**

Icing (powdered) sugar, for dusting

Prepare batter. In a bowl, combine flour, baking soda, egg and water. Stir until mixture is smooth.

Heat oil for deep-frying over medium heat.

Dip bananas in batter and let excess batter drip.

Lower banana halves gently into hot oil one by one so they do not stick. Cook in batches until golden brown and crisp. Remove and drain well on paper towels.

Dust with icing sugar before serving.

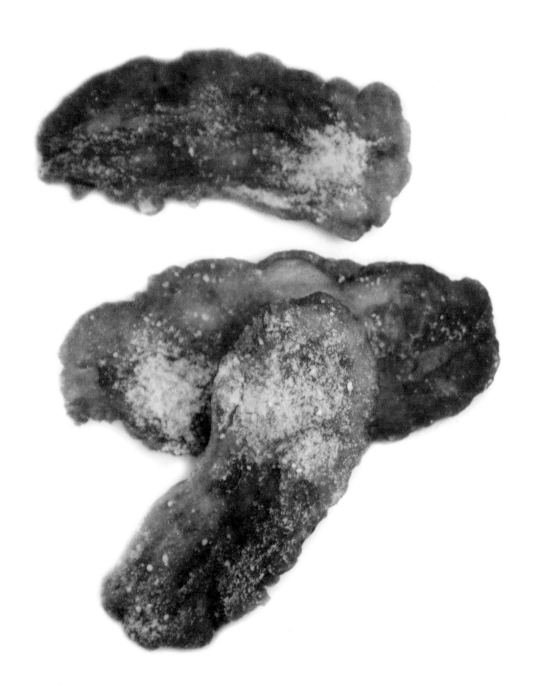

MAJA BLANCA COCONUT AND CORN CUSTARD

SERVES 4

1^1/$_2$ **cups coconut milk**

^{1}/$_2$ **cup cornflour**

^{3}/$_4$ **cup coconut cream**

^{1}/$_2$ **cup cream of corn**

^{3}/$_4$ **cup whole corn kernels**

^{1}/$_2$ **cup sugar**

Fried coconut milk curd (*latik*), page 92 or toasted desiccated coconut, to garnish

In a bowl, stir together coconut milk and cornflour. Mix well.

Add coconut cream, cream of corn, corn kernels and sugar. Stir to mix.

Transfer to a pot and place over medium heat. Cook, stirring continuously until mixture is thick and pudding-like.

Pour into a greased 20 x 20-cm pan. Cover and leave to cool and set.

When set, slice and top with fried coconut milk curd or toasted desiccated coconut.

Serve.

LECHE FLAN
MILK CUSTARD
SERVES 4

3 Tbsp + 1 Tbsp sugar
4 large eggs
300 ml sweetened condensed milk
$^3/_4$ cup water

Place 3 Tbsp sugar in a large oval-shaped aluminium flan pan and caramelise over low to medium heat, moving the pan around with a pair of tongs to distribute evenly.

Remove from heat and set aside to harden.

In a bowl, beat eggs with a whisk.

Add condensed milk, water and remaining 1 Tbsp sugar.
Stir until combined.

Pass the mixture through cheesecloth and pour into flan pan with hardened caramel.

Set flan pan over a hot water bath (bain marie) and heat for 30 minutes or until custard is firm. Set aside to cool.

To unmould, pass a knife around the edge of flan and overturn onto a serving plate.

Serve.

BIKO STICKY RICE CAKE

SERVES 4

1 cup glutinous rice, washed and drained
$^1/_2$ cup fresh coconut water
1 cup coconut milk
$^3/_4$ cup brown sugar
2 cups coconut cream

Place glutinous rice in a pot and add coconut water and coconut milk. Bring to the boil over medium heat, then lower heat to a simmer, stirring occasionally.

When rice begins to become dense and thick, add sugar and stir to dissolve.

When mixture becomes very thick, transfer to a greased 20 x 20-cm pan and set aside to cool.

In the meantime, prepare fried coconut milk curd (*latik*). Bring coconut cream to a boil in a pan, stirring occasionally until liquid thickens and oil starts to appear.

At this point, start to stir continuously, scraping the bottom of the pan, until curd turns golden brown. Remove from heat and drain fried curd of oil.

Top rice cake with fried coconut milk curd.

Slice to serve.

BUKO PANDAN SALAD
COCONUT AND PANDAN SALAD

SERVES 4

180 g unsweetened green gelatin powder

3 cups fresh coconut water

1 pandan leaf, cleaned and knotted

2 young coconuts, flesh extracted and cut into strips

1 cup (all-purpose) cream

3 Tbsp sweetened condensed milk

Place gelatin powder, coconut water and pandan leaf in a pot over low to medium heat, stirring until gelatin is dissolved and mixture starts to simmer. Remove and discard pandan leaf.

Transfer gelatin mixture to greased 20 x 15-cm pan and set aside to cool and set.

When gelatin is set, cut into cubes and place in a salad bowl. Add coconut flesh to bowl.

In a small bowl, stir together cream and condensed milk and add to salad bowl. Toss to mix.

Cover and refrigerate. Serve chilled.